D1458461

A Book for a Cunt.

Some people should be dipped in vagisil, then they wouldn't be such irritating cunts.

It's better to let someone think you are a cunt, than open your mouth and prove it.

Is your ass jealous of the amount of shit that comes out of your mouth?

You must have been born on the highway, because that's where most accidents happen.

The only way you are ever getting laid is if you crawl up a chicken's ass.

I'm jealous of all the people who haven't met you.

Your name is enough to piss me off.

I hope one day you choke on the shit you talk.

Someone out there loves you. Not me. I think you are a cunt.

When I think of you I touch myself. I rub my temples because you give me a fucking migraine.

You are a cunt, ain't no medicine for that shit.

Someday you will go far, and I hope you will stay there.

I may not be perfect, but at least I'm not a cunt like you.

No need to repeat yourself. I ignored you fine the first time.

I heard you got your left side cut off. Now you're all right.

Light travels faster than sound. This is why you appear bright until we hear you speak.

Remember when you ate that clock? Was so time consuming.

Remember when I smacked you in the head with a can of soda? You were lucky it was a soft drink you cunt.

When I listen to you, I wonder who ties your shoe laces up for you.

I don't have a short temper, I have a quick reaction to your bullshit.

Looks like its 'fuck this shit o' clock.' Bye cunt.

In case you didn't hear
the look I just gave you,
SHUT UP.

People say you act like you don't give a fuck. You are not acting, you are just a cunt.

The trash gets picked up tomorrow. Be ready cunt.

You are fat and I'm not going to sugar coat it because you will eat that too.

Of course I talk like a cunt, how else would you understand me?

There is a glass full of 'shut the fuck up' on the table, why don't you have some?

Two wrongs don't make a right, ask your parents.

You sound reasonable, it must be time to up my medication.

Your birth certificate is an apology letter from the condom factory.

What language are you speaking? Because it sounds like bullshit.

Don't you just love nature, despite what it did to you?

You are the reason the gene pool needs a lifeguard.

Most people live and learn. You just live.

You have the perfect face for the radio.

I've met some pricks, but you are a fucking cactus.

You smell like drama and a headache, please get away from me.

Ignore the fake smile, I'd punch you in the throat if I wouldn't lose my job over it.

When I say, 'have a nice day', remember the 'cunt' is silent.

When you don't like someone, so they assume its because you are jealous of them. Nope, I think you are a cunt believe it or not.

If being a cunt was a career option, you would be set for life.

When people say you are a nice person when they get to know you, they mean you are a cunt and they got used to it.

You are welcome!

Printed in Great Britain
by Amazon

74120535R10028